Lessons from the Republicans

Tim Hames is a political writer for *The Times* and a former lecturer in Politics for Christ Church and Oriel Colleges, Oxford. He specialises in British and American politics – notably the contemporary Republican and Conservative parties – and comparative government.
His publications include *A Conservative Revolution: The Reagan-Thatcher decade in perspective* (joint editor) and *Governing America* (joint author).

Alan Grant is Senior Lecturer in Politics at Oxford Brookes University. He specialises in American Government but also writes on aspects of British politics especially local government.
His publications include *The American Political Process* and *Contemporary American Politics*.
He served as a member of Buckinghamshire County Council for twelve years, was leader of the Conservative group and stood as a parliamentary candidate in 1987.

Lessons from the Republicans

TIM HAMES & ALAN GRANT

The Social Market Foundation
June 1997

First published by The Social Market Foundation 1997
in association with Profile Books Ltd

The Social Market Foundation
20 Queen Anne's Gate
London SW1H 9AA

Profile Books
62 Queen Anne Street
London W1M 9LA

Printed in Great Britain by Redwood Books

A CIP catalogue record for this book is available from the British Library

Paper No. 31

ISBN 1 874097 81 X

Contents

Acknowledgements

The authors would like to thank Julia and Sarah
for their patience during the progress of this project.
Both are grateful to Rick Nye and all at
the Social Market Foundation for the speed and efficiency
with which an initial idea became a final product.

Foreword

Throughout the 1980s Britain was very much a net exporter of public policy ideas. In the 1990s the terms of trade have been reversed. Increasingly, politicians from across the political spectrum have looked to America for inspiration.

The debt owed by the new government to the style and substance of the Clinton Administration is well known, but less attention has been paid to what the Conservatives can learn from Republican attempts to rebuild and reinvigorate themselves in the wake of Clinton's victory in 1992.

In September 1994, the SMF published a memorandum by Daniel Finkelstein which examined the experience of the Republican Party after nearly two years in opposition. He concluded that its time out of office had brought it no intellectual dividend. The task of synthesising the distinct strands of American conservatism into an intellectually coherent and politically appealing message still lay ahead.

Two months later, when the Republicans engineered a landslide which brought them control of Congress for the first time in over forty years, this seemed a misjudgement. Many assumed this extraordinary feat was the harbinger of a Republican revolution which would sweep President Clinton from office. But despite some legislative successes, that revolution has stopped short of the White House.

What then can British Conservatives learn from the Republicans' experience? In this paper, Tim Hames and Alan Grant look at the policies and principles which lay behind the 'Contract with America', the first national manifesto in the history of American politics on which the Republican Party fought and won those Congressional elections of 1994.

In particular they examine what the Contract says about economic policy, crime and welfare reform in the light of a 'New' Democrat president; how successful the Republicans were in turning their agenda into law and what conclusions Conservatives might draw as they attempt to provide an effective opposition to 'New' Labour.

All manner of advice will be offered to the new Conservative leader about the direction which his party must now take. Hames's and Grant's analysis is a timely and valuable contribution to the process of reconstruction that is just beginning.

Roderick Nye
June 1997

Introduction

Political ideas come from many sources and often are borrowed from abroad. In most areas of intellectual and political life, the United States has been the powerhouse of ideas throughout this century. This is as true for the social sciences as it has been for the natural sciences. Today, at a time when both major political parties in Britain have, for different reasons and to varying degrees, apparently exhausted much of what sustained them in the 1970s and 1980s, it is understandable that they should look across the Atlantic to the United States for inspiration.

However, all ideas are not equally transferable. While the United States and Britain share much in terms of language and a common intellectual tradition there are substantial differences in both the structure of government and the nature of the two societies. These must be taken into account before enthusiastic reformers import particular ideas. Much of this paper will be devoted to analysis of the practical applicability as well as the political attractiveness of recent American policy innovation.

The two main parties in Britain may disagree about many issues, but both seem willing to accept the United States as a role model. This is especially striking for New Labour. Not only was their electoral strategy openly borrowed from Bill Clinton and the Democratic Party but also much of the impetus behind the Blair prospectus. The notion of education/training and 'welfare to work' as the big idea that would reshape the British economy has a distinctly familiar feel to it. The idea of reinventing government through public/private partnership also seems to carry with it a 'Made in America' label. In its first few weeks of office, Labour's new chancellor has proposed reforming the Bank of England along the lines of the Federal Reserve Board and transforming the regulatory regime in the City of London to create an imitation of the Securities and Exchange Commission. The home secretary has suggested the introduction of district attorneys and a 'Drugs Czar', ideas clearly modelled on the American originals. It has been less 'New Labour, New Britain' than 'New Labour, New York'.

Labour's election manifesto, however, was admirably bipartisan. Tony Blair borrowed the concept of a contract from Newt Gingrich and much of its policy content from the Clinton administration. The vast majority of the political ideas imported by Labour originates from the New Democrat branch of the American policy debate. They include a number of themes in the economic and education spheres previously associated with former Clinton Labour Secretary Robert Reich, many of which have not been implemented in the United States. The remaining small proportion of policy innovations that have different parentage comes from Australia. Indeed, it is very curious that the Labour government goes to such lengths to stress its pro-European inclinations when its own manifesto is such a testament to the continued power of ideas from the English-speaking world.

Nevertheless, while the links between Labour and the Democrats have been explored in great depth, and certainly merit further analysis, they will not be the primary focus of this paper. Instead we will look at Republican policy activity, notably at the congressional level, and assess how it might best be interpreted by those Conservatives inclined to sympathise with all or part of it. Our focus is justified by two observations. First, since the landmark American elections of 1994, the Republicans have dominated both the chambers of Congress and a substantial majority of the largest states. For the last two years, the story of American public life at all levels has been the struggle to implement a radical conservative prospectus. Second, the scale of the defeat that engulfed the Conservative Party in May 1997 should prompt a wholesale reassessment of its philosophy and policy; just as the loss of the Presidency in 1992 – after a twelve-year occupancy of the White House – forced Republicans back to the intellectual drawing board. It is a reasonable assumption that many Conservatives will become extremely interested in the American agenda over the coming months and years. The main aspect of their interest will be the Contract with America that has formed the core of the Republican project in Washington. This will be our centrepiece as well.

1: The Contract with America: Concept, Content and Consequences

The Concept

The very concept of the Contract with America, regardless of its content, was an act of breathtaking political daring. In Britain, the notion of a formal party document outlining a proposed legislative programme, which a party would implement if elected, is a regular feature of all elections. The manifesto and the allied idea of a mandate for that manifesto from electoral victory is so commonplace that were any other political party to suggest campaigning without one it would cause an uproar.

In the United States, the opposite has invariably been the case. The separation of powers between the President, House of Representatives and Senate alongside the historic tendency of the two main parties to act as loose regional coalitions, rather than philosophically defined enterprises, has always mitigated against a manifesto. For most of this century such an enterprise would have been considered foolish. Candidates for a political party would be unlikely to seek such a set of formal commitments. And even if this kind of document could be created there would be little possibility of holding elected officials to its provisions once the votes had been counted.

It is true that presidential nominating conventions, held every four years, do adopt statements of policy — known as platforms — that are frequently fought over by party activists. However, these have been seen as broad indicators of party preferences on issues of the day and have been regarded as binding on either presidential candidates or other candidates for election. In practice, they are tailored to suit the individual priorities of the likely nominee rather than expressions of a collective party inclination, let alone a legislative schedule.

The only partial exception to this occurred in the 1980 campaign. On that occasion, candidate Ronald Reagan and many Republican congressional aspirants stood together on the steps of Congress and promised to introduce a 30 per cent cut in income tax rates if elected. Significantly, among the most enthusiastic supporters of this novel display on the House side was one very junior member, Representative Newt Gingrich. This symbolic moment of unity was widely dismissed as a gimmick by the American media. However, Reagan was elected, a very large tax cut (25 per cent) was indeed proposed, all congressional Republicans who had attended the press 'stunt' duly supported the measure and it was passed and signed into law. Nonetheless, it was a one-off event on a single and immensely popular issue. It was not repeated during the 1984 Reagan re-election campaign nor in any other contest before the 1994 Republican triumph.

The reasons why the Republicans adopted the Contract are numerous and in the main are not relevant to Britain. The Contract reflected the increasing degree of (conservative) ideological convergence among Republicans across the United States. It was also a response to the growing cynicism and alienation of the American public to conventional politicians in all forms, best illustrated by the 19 per cent share of the popular vote Ross Perot achieved in the 1992 presidential election. In characterising the programme as a Contract with the American people, House Republicans promised to hold an open debate and free vote on each of the proposals and argued that if they failed to live up to their pledge then the voters should hold them to account at the next election. Ultimately, it was a device which ensured that when Republicans did eventually recapture the House of Representatives (for the first time in forty years) internal power could be centralised in the hands of the new speaker rather than (as had usually been the case in the United States) dispersed towards the key congressional committees.

Two key factors about the Contract with America should be noted by British observers at this stage:

1. There is no novelty in the concept. Republican strategists acknowledged they had borrowed the idea from Britain and had done so with the deliberate aim of making the House of Representatives operate in a disciplined, party-oriented fashion similar to the House of Commons.

2. There is no reliable evidence that the creation of the Contract in itself won votes for the Republican Party or can explain the nature of their triumph in November 1994. Individual parts of the Contract – on economic policy, welfare reform and crime – were widely emphasised by candidates and clearly influenced the electorate, but the Contract as a collective entity was not a crucial element.

The Content

The importance of the Contract lay in its radicalism. Republicans decided that five principles – individual liberty, economic opportunity, limited government, personal responsibility and security at home and abroad – would form the basis of their philosophy and would be central to the vision they would communicate to the electorate. It is these policy issues rather than the concept of the Contract that should influence the British political debate.

The Contract consisted of a prologue and ten specific proposals some of which would require more than one legislative act to implement. These can be briefly summarised as follows:

THE PROLOGUE involved the adoption of one new law and seven alterations in the rules of the House of Representatives. The emphasis was upon modernising the manner in which the House operated (allowing the minority party more opportunities to influence debate) and removing aspects of 'sleaze' that had been associated with the institution during the long period of Democratic hegemony. The major aspect affecting policy substance was a rule change to the effect that a 60 per cent majority would be required to pass tax increases. As the rule could be overturned by simple majority this was a mostly symbolic shift.

THE FISCAL RESPONSIBILITY ACT was divided into two parts. The first was a constitutional amendment that would mandate a balanced budget as the American economic norm. The second was a legislative change that would allow the President greater authority to challenge unnecessary public spending.

THE TAKING BACK OUR STREETS ACT outlined a mass of Republican anti-crime legislation.

THE PERSONAL RESPONSIBILITY ACT covered the Republican proposals for welfare reform.

THE FAMILY REINFORCEMENT ACT brought together a set of 'pro-family' tax credits, together with more stringent measures to ensure financial contributions from absent parents as well as tougher punishments towards crimes committed against children.

THE AMERICAN DREAM RESTORATION ACT was the showcase set of cuts in taxation promised by the Republicans.

THE NATIONAL SECURITY RESTORATION ACT pledged to reverse the trend towards cuts in defence spending and set new priorities in American foreign policy.

THE SENIOR CITIZENS EQUITY ACT comprised a set of tax changes designed to appeal to elderly voters that mostly reversed measures passed by President Clinton and the Democratic-controlled Congress in 1993.

THE JOB CREATION AND WAGE ENHANCEMENT ACT combined a large cut in capital gains taxation with a substantial assault on government regulatory power over business.

THE COMMON SENSE LEGAL REFORM ACT pledged a comprehensive overhaul of the American legal system aimed at reducing the number of legal cases.

THE CITIZENS LEGISLATURE ACT responded to a widespread movement at state level which favoured capping the number of terms politicians can serve in office. It promised to introduce a constitutional amendment mandating limits on congressional careers.

Much, indeed most, of the Contract with America has little or no applicability to British politics. The prologue is concerned with the internal structure of the House of Representatives and, while the broad theme of institutional reform may have a value in the United Kingdom, the detail does not. The Fiscal Responsibility Act largely affects the machinery by which American economic policy is made. As there is no written constitution in the United Kingdom and the methods by which we make fiscal decisions are different to those in the United States, the proposal is irrelevant this side of the Atlantic.

Many other aspects are also irrelevant. The National Security Restoration Act refers to distinct American features of foreign and defence policy. The Senior Citizens Equity Act largely consisted of measures to countermand previous legislation, associated with Bill Clinton, that do not have parallels in Britain. The Common Sense Legal Reform Act – although an admirable piece of legislation – was shaped by the astonishing power of the legal profession in America. While the law and lawyers are becoming more significant in Britain, the scale does not compare with the United States; the reasons behind the change in Britain are rather different and so, one suspects, would be the policy response. The Citizens Legislature Act and the limits to terms of office were born out of the apparent ability of incumbent legislators at all levels to make themselves almost invulnerable to the threat of electoral defeat. After 1 May 1997 this would not seem to be a major dilemma afflicting the British body politic.

However, one theme underlying many of the proposals was a desire to reduce the power of 'Big Government' and the federal bureaucracy, and devolve power to the states and local governments which are closer to the people. Although this was not carried through with perfect consistency, the idea that decentralisation of power brings major advantages to both democracy and effective delivery of services is one British Conservatives would do well to consider.

One of the legacies of the eighteen years of Conservative government is a more centralised state where local authorities have lost control of many of their powers to non-elected quangos, and the discretion they can exercise over their remaining responsibilities has been reduced as a result of budget capping. Not only has this deprived voters of any real choice between the parties at local elections but it has had a disastrous impact on Conservative representation in local government and contributed to the decline of the Tory Party at the grass roots level.

British Conservatives should see elected local government not only as a check on an overpowerful centre but also as having the potential to function as a laboratory of democracy where experimental policy initiatives might be tested for the benefit of the political system as a whole. As we shall see, one of the great strengths of American democray is the way new approaches to public policy problems can be tested at a state or local level and, if successful, adapted to the needs of other states or taken up at a national level.

Three policy domains within the Contract are particularly interesting to compare:

1. Economic measures contained predominantly in the American Dream Restoration Act but also in provisions of the Family Reinforcement Act and the Job Creation and Wage Enhancement Act.

2. Welfare reform promoted by the Personal Responsibility Act and to a lesser extent by the Family Reinforcement Act.

3. Measures to deal with crime, chiefly outlined by the Taking Back our Streets Act and sections of the Family Reinforcement Act.

The Consequences

Before embarking on a more substantive examination of the economic, welfare and crime measures proposed in the United States, and their applicability to the British context, it is worth considering the political fate of the Contract and congressional Republicans.

The Contract was introduced with a burst of activity. The House of Representatives passed every aspect, except the constitutional endorsement of term limits, in a ninety-one-day blitz. In the same period, however, the Senate passed only two minor measures and failed (by one vote) to back the balanced budget amendment. After that, political attention focused on the ambitious plans of the Republican majority to produce a balanced budget by the year 2002 without the requirement being placed in the Constitution itself. President Clinton made numerous concessions on both the principle of this proposal and its timetable. However, he opposed any provisions that would reduce the rate of future growth in health care spending for the elderly (Medicare) and the poor (Medicaid). Democrats accused Republicans of abandoning these programmes in order to permit enormous tax cuts for the rich. The federal government suffered two partial closures during the political struggle that followed.

When it became apparent that the president had won the war of public relations, the Republicans backed down and licked their wounds. They abandoned the seven-year balanced budget proposal and, temporarily at least, the attempt to reconstruct the major entitlement programmes the United States has enjoyed for some thirty years but which have been a major source of its fiscal difficulties. Instead they produced a 9 per cent cut in spending for those parts of the budget they could directly influence (discretionary domestic expenditure). This in turn required concessions to Clinton in order to ensure his agreement.

From there, the Republicans cherry-picked the more popular aspects of the Contract and adopted other measures to ensure their political recovery and re-election in November 1996. Welfare reform (rather than health care reform) became their predominant concern. The Republicans presented legislation President Clinton felt politically obliged to accept, even though it meant abandoning positions long associated with the Democratic Party. That success, when added to bipartisan proposals on making the transfer of health insurance easier for those moving jobs, plus the re-authorisation of the major environmental programmes, greatly assisted the Republican Party. It essentially ensured their re-election. In May 1997 they revisited the budget terrain that had caused so much grief fifteen months earlier. On this occasion a booming economy and substantial compromise permitted a deal to be struck with Bill Clinton.

The ultimate fate of the Contract with America can be categorised in three ways. The first includes those measures that were never accepted by the Senate after passage in the House of Representatives. The most notable elements were in the balanced budget amendment and National Security Restoration Act. The second comprises proposals passed by Congress but then blocked by the presidential veto. These included the Job Creation and Wage Enhancement Act; the Common Sense Legal Reform Act; the initial version of the Personal Responsibility Act and the first Republican budget, which contained much of the American Dream Restoration Act, the Family Reinforcement Act and Senior Citizens Equity Act.

The third category consists of those provisions which, after considerable compromise with President Clinton, entered American law. These included the parts of the Fiscal Responsibility Act that strengthened presidential power over the budget; the final version of welfare reform; strands of the anti-crime legislation and one section of the Common Sense Legal Reform Act where Congress mustered the two-thirds margin necessary to overturn Bill Clinton's veto. It now appears the bipartisan compact reached on the budget will meet the Republican objective of fiscal equilibrium by the year 2002 and (in a highly diluted form) will finally allow much of the American Dream Restoration Act, Family Reinforcement Act and Senior Citizens Equity Act to reach the statute book. All in all, a mixed record – but one that has had a substantial impact on American politics.

There are certainly cautionary messages here about radicalism and the dangers of circumvention that a Conservative government in Britain would be wise to heed. On the whole though, the fate of the Contract in the legislative process reflects distinctive features of the American Constitution that have no equivalent in British politics. They are:

• The rules of the Senate which often require 60 per cent approval (and hence cross-party co-operation) to prevail over a minority filibuster (a commonly used obstruction technique). The upper chamber is unlikely to prove such a problem in the United Kingdom.

• The veto power vested in the head of state. This power, used with devastating effect in the United States, is again unlikely to prove troublesome in the United Kingdom in the absence of an extraordinary change in behaviour by Her Majesty the Queen.

• Eternal elections. The entire House of Representatives and one-third of the Senate has to stand for election every two years. This creates a hypersensitivity to public opinion and cautions against necessary but unpopular proposals.

Under Britain's system of government the implementation of those parts of the Contract thought worthy of transfer would be much more straightforward. The question of what might be considered both desirable and practicable – in economics, welfare and crime – is the core of what follows.

2: Can Policy Cross the Atlantic?

The next three sections follow the same formula. First we outline the content of the original Republican agenda and, where relevant, look briefly at which parts have become American law. Then we discuss whether and how far some or all of the policies could be adjusted to the circumstances of the United Kingdom. Finally, we draw some conclusions for the Conservative Party.

The Economic Agenda: Radical but Possible

Republican plans for tax reform were far from incremental. The three basic provisions of the American Dream Restoration Act were:

1. A $500 FAMILY TAX CREDIT. This would reduce tax demands by $500 per child for all families earning less than $200,000. In practice, around 90 per cent of those eligible earn $75,000 or less and are considered middle-class rather than wealthy. The emphasis on the family reflected Republican concern about the erosion of the family and the influence of the Christian right within American conservative ranks.

2. REFORM OF THE MARRIAGE PENALTY. The complicated operating arrangements of the federal tax system in the United States often means that married couples are better off in tax terms as two individuals living together. The bill proposed spending up to $2 billion annually in order to eliminate this anomaly.

3. THE EXPANSION OF TAX-FREE INDIVIDUAL SAVINGS ACCOUNTS. This allowed Americans to save and then spend

up to $2,000 a year, without being taxed, provided the monies were used for retirement income, purchase of a first home, education expenses or medical costs.

The other parts of the Contract which also affected economic policy were as follows:

- THE FAMILY REINFORCEMENT ACT suggested a tax credit of up to $5,000 for the costs incurred during the lengthy child adoption process. This benefit would diminish if incomes approached $60,000. The bill also proposed a $500 refundable tax credit for individuals who looked after a parent or grandparent in their own home.
- THE SENIOR CITIZENS EQUITY ACT favoured increasing the amounts the elderly could earn before they lost part of their pension entitlement. It also reduced the tax burden on incomes of older people. In addition, Republicans wanted to increase tax incentives for private insurance cover for long-term illness and nursing care.
- THE JOB CREATION AND WAGE ENHANCEMENT ACT proposed an effective cut of 50 per cent in the rate of capital gains taxation. In the future, capital gains would be linked to inflation, thus further cutting the actual amount paid. A host of additional incentives rewarding investment were offered to small businesses. The power of federal regulatory agencies to impose bureaucratic burdens on business would be attacked not only by a direct assault on individual regulations but also by introducing new principles into the entire process. Federal agencies would be required, in public, to conduct a cost-benefit analysis of proposed rules, identify the

bill that would be imposed on the corporate sector and then justify that imposition to Congress.

In addition to the formal economic agenda of the Contract, Republican politicians focused on three other major topics which have not yet reached their legislative zenith. They are:

1. THE FLAT TAX – OR MUCH FLATTER TAX. This proposal would grant Americans a generous set of personal allowances and then charge one single 'flat' rate of taxation afterwards. Although it is mostly associated with the presidential candidature of Steve Forbes, its real political parent was Representative Richard Armey of Texas, the Majority Leader of the House of Representatives (in effect Gringrich's deputy). Certain Republicans deemed even this approach unduly incremental. Representative Bill Archer, chairman of the influential House Ways and Means Committee, favours the repeal of the federal income tax and the introduction of a consumption tax in its place.

2. A RADICAL SIMPLIFICATION OF THE TAX SYSTEM. Even those not entirely convinced by the flat tax favoured the elimination of the seven million word long American tax code. It would be replaced by a small set of personal allowances (such as the family tax credit), permitting the average American taxpayer to file their returns on a form little larger than a postcard.

3. THE EFFECTIVE ELIMINATION OF INHERITANCE TAXES. By the beginning of 1997 Republicans were increasingly enthusiastic for a plan that would raise the level at which

inheritance taxes would start to be paid, to a point where 95 per cent of the population were excluded. The figure of $600,000 (£400,000) was particularly popular although some were in favour of an even higher threshold.

Relatively few of these ideas became law in their original form. The main deregulation measure was vetoed. Bill Clinton adopted the credits associated with the Family Reinforcement Act, and it seems the 1997 compromise on the budget will allow a highly restricted form of family tax credit, a substantial cut in capital gains taxes and some reform of inheritance tax to take place. The overall changes implicit in the bipartisan package would produce a fall in tax revenues of some $250 billion over ten years, provided the federal budget remains in balance. This means a final prediction of the Republican impact is almost impossible.

LESSONS FOR BRITAIN

Conservatives in Britain should certainly take an interest in the economic agenda of the Republicans. Although there are obvious differences in the physical size, population and *per capita* income of the United States and the United Kingdom, the two nations have enough in common for an assumption of comparability. To some extent this has always been true but the comparison has been made sharper by the impact of privatisation and supply-side reforms begun by Margaret Thatcher and advanced in certain cases by John Major.

The structure of the British economy is now more explicitly capitalist than twenty years ago. As a result of the radical privatisation programme introduced by the Conservatives it now has rather more in common with the American economy, and rather less with the capitalist/corporatist mix associated with Europe. Mrs Thatcher's willingness to allow much of manufacturing industry to be reorganised and rationalised in the 1980s means that in both Britain and America the economic emphasis is now firmly on the service sector. It does not seem the election of a Labour government threatens to alter these elements of economic convergence.

The proportion of all economic activity absorbed by the state, in terms of public spending, is still larger in Britain (at around 40 per cent) than in the United States (roughly 30 per cent for all levels of government combined). The same is true for the total tax burden. However, here Britain has clearly taken a path that again is different from the European social democratic model. Unless policy in the United Kingdom changes dramatically under Labour then it will remain the case that British politicians look to America for inspiration in economic matters. To date the behaviour of Tony Blair and Gordon Brown towards the New Democrat prospectus suggests they share this presumption. Labour markets remain more flexible in the United States than Britain but once again the Thatcher effect has reduced the difference between the two nations and highlighted the fact that Britain is much closer to the American than the European norm.

The similarity between the two countries is also due in part to such matters as the coincidence in the general pattern of the business cycle and the linkage in stock market trends and even foreign exchange movements. All this suggests that while the specifics of American legislation, especially on tax, should not be translated verbatim into British law, the principles behind such specifics would lend themselves to adaptation by Conservatives.

The lessons of the American experience highlight a number of ideas:

• Partly for the benefits of simplicity, Conservatives should consider creating a single basic rate of income tax at 20 per cent even if it is only achieved by redistribution within the present overall tax take. However, once this happens, a much greater emphasis could be placed on tax allowances not merely by increasing the existing personal allowances but also by adopting new allowances, tied to specific policy objectives such as the preservation of the family or rewarding certain areas of private expenditure.

• The Republicans switched from an emphasis on tax rates to tax credits. They did this for two reasons relevant to British Conservatives. First, once marginal rates are forced below a certain level, it becomes impossible to offer further cuts which are radical and appeal to the electorate (unless income tax is abolished entirely). In the United States once the basic rate had fallen to 15 per cent (as it did in 1986) the rate-cutting agenda ran out of political steam. Second, the enhanced tax credits allowed Republicans to steer resources to areas popular with the American public, such as support for the family. In contrast to the Democrats who favoured direct state expenditure in these areas, the Republican approach was to encourage (via tax inducement) more private resources to be devoted to the same priorities. As commentators in the United States suggest, the creation of a small number of very particular (and popular) tax allowances can combine with the abolition of virtually all other existing loopholes and anomalies to simplify the system of personal taxation enormously.

• A concentration of allowances also permits tax cuts and the introduction of a flat tax rate to be brought together. In Britain both the basic and top rates of tax start on relatively low levels of income. Assuming a dual rate structure (20 per cent and 40 per cent), a ruthless concentration of allowances would enable large numbers of poorer people to be excluded from the tax system altogether – a development that could hardly be described as regressive. If the top rate of tax in the United Kingdom did not start to operate until income reached a higher level than at present (for example £40,000 or £50,000 per annum) then a clear majority of those currently paying tax in that band would be excluded. The precise outcome would inevitably depend on the point chosen for the top rate, but the net effect would be to create a *de facto* flat tax as the vast majority of British taxpayers would sit within the 20 per cent band. The different distribution of income in Britain makes an effective flat tax easier to achieve than in the United States.

• Similarly, a lower threshold than the one in the United States for the payment of inheritance tax – for example on estates valued at £250,000 and above – would also mean the effective abolition of this form of taxation for the vast majority of households in Britain.

• If the new Republican emphasis in personal taxation, with its stress on 'pro-family' allowances rather than incremental reductions in basic rates, holds some appeal for

British Conservatives, then there is also room for manoeuvre on business tax matters as well. This area has not been seriously addressed since the innovations introduced by Nigel Lawson which, at the time, made the corporate taxation system in the United Kingdom among the most imaginative in the world. By the year 2002, nearly twenty years will have past since Lawson's welcome radicalism. That alone would suggest a fresh look is now justified. The overwhelming objective of the Job Creation and Wage Replacement Act was to produce a tax regime that was biased towards pro-growth investment rather than sophisticated accountancy practice. This worthwhile objective would require different forms of legislation in the United Kingdom but it illustrates the guiding principle. Britain, and the European Union, might also benefit from the public accountability ideas that the Republicans favoured introducing into regulatory affairs.

In short, the character of the American and British economies and the nature of the policy ideas reflected in the Contract with America and elsewhere, would allow British policy reformers to look west with some confidence that what they saw could be successfully placed in a British setting. Indeed, there are very few aspects of recent Republican thinking on taxation and regulation that would not be worth close examination by the Conservative Party.

Welfare Reform: Handle with Care

Few aspects of the American agenda have been examined with greater interest by both the left and right in Britain than welfare reform. In 1992 Bill Clinton was elected promising to 'end welfare as we know it'. He did not and to his subsequent regret he engaged in the unsuccessful pursuit of health care reform instead. Republicans swept into office in 1994 determined to definitively end welfare as it had been understood since the New Deal administration of Franklin D. Roosevelt. Their plans outlined in the Personal Responsibility Act involved:

- ANTI-ILLEGITIMACY PROVISIONS. A central aim was to reduce the numbers of teenage pregnancies and illegitimate births for those already on welfare. Republicans planned to withhold payments of AFDC (Aid to Families with Dependent Children, which since 1935 has been the chief means of support for poor households headed by a single person) and housing benefit to all mothers under the age of eighteen. States would be free to extend this ceiling up to the age of twenty-one. All monies saved would be sent back to the states in the form of block grants for services (not cash) to be provided to these mothers. Those between the ages of eighteen and twenty either had to marry or reside in the parental home in order to receive AFDC in the states which did not decide to raise the age ceiling. No mother in receipt of AFDC, regardless of her age, would receive additional benefits if she had more illegitimate children.

- STRONGER WORK REQUIREMENTS. In the continuation of well-established Republican support for 'workfare', states were to be encouraged to create their own education and training schemes aimed at moving people from welfare to paid employment as quickly as possible. Such programmes had to involve at least thirty-five hours of work-related activity and last a maximum of two years. At that point AFDC would usually be stopped. Furthermore, all states were required to end AFDC payments to families that had received a total of five years' worth of welfare cheques – regardless of any other factor.

• SPENDING CAPS. The bill created maximum amounts for expenditure on welfare, tied to the rate of inflation and the overall growth in population. The principle of welfare as an automatic entitlement would cease. A large number of specific grants for welfare purposes, such as food stamps and free school lunches, would be consolidated into block grants which states could use as they saw appropriate.

• STATES FLEXIBILITY. States would be granted greater freedom over how they used AFDC resources. For example, they could offer lower levels of benefits if the recipient had not completed a high-school education or if they had recently moved from a different state.

The Republicans in the House of Representatives succeeded in passing welfare reform on their own terms twice – once as free-standing legislation and then as part of their balanced budget package. Even then substantial compromise was required on the aspects on illegitimacy to save the proposal from defeat in the Senate. On both occasions President Clinton issued a veto and the measure was lost. In 1996, Republicans returned to the subject in the heat of an election campaign. They offered further concessions designed to satisfy conservative Democrats. Although the final legislation still offended most Democrats,

President Clinton did not want to cast a third veto against a popular proposal and so he signed the bill.

The third and final draft of the Personal Responsibility and Work Opportunity Reconciliation Act in 1996 toned down most of the provisions mandating states to act against illegitimacy. However, it did end the sixty-one-year old federal government guarantee of welfare payments for all eligible low-income mothers and children. Funds would now be sent to the states which would have enormous power over the final distribution. Several important new federal restrictions would apply: welfare recipients would be required to work within two years of first receiving benefits and they would be limited to a total of five years on welfare. Provision for immigrants – both legal and illegal – was cut sharply. Savings reaching nearly $55 billion over seven years were forecast. This was a political compromise but in contrast with other aspects of the Contract with America. There was little dispute that President Clinton had conceded more than the Republicans.

LESSONS FOR BRITAIN

Conservatives in the United Kingdom might well be tempted by the welfare reform proposals the Republicans in Washington not only designed but largely succeeded in implementing. But they would be advised to proceed with caution despite their enthusiasm for ideas advanced at the federal level or, for that matter, similar notions pioneered in many of America's largest states.

Unlike their respective economies, the structures and cultures affecting the American and British welfare systems are highly distinctive and comparison is far from easy. This is more important than the widespread perception that many welfare problems – especially the dependency culture – appear to be shared on both sides of the Atlantic.

The many dissimilarities between the two welfare structures start with the larger element of private or philanthropic provision as a proportion of total welfare spending that exists in the United States. The American welfare system consists of distinct layers and partnership arrangements between the national, state and local levels that do not exist in Britain. The principle of universal benefits (at least for those under sixty-five) has never been firmly established in the United States. The ideals of socialism (even social democracy) or redistribution of income have also not been taken up. Instead the American welfare system proceeds by selecting certain sections of society Americans have long considered worthy of support and distributing federal dollars directly to them. These groups include veterans (those who have served in the United States Armed Forces), the elderly, the disabled and children from single-parent households. This last group was brought into the public system in the 1930s when it comprised principally widows with children (or deserted wives) whose savings had been eliminated during the Depression.

Many of these groups are not particularly poor. Taken as a whole, the elderly in the United States, who benefit from Social Security (pensions in the British context) and Medicare (health care coverage heavily subsidised by the taxpayer), are disproportionately wealthy. With the exception of these two programmes for those over sixty-five, the middle class is largely excluded from the American welfare system in a manner that is not true in Britain. If health care is included as part of social welfare then the difference between the two nations becomes even starker. The American middle-class does not benefit from publicly sponsored health provision until after retirement. The majority of their compatriots in Britain rely predominantly or exclusively on the National Health Service. As for the poor, in the United States a large proportion of welfare benefits has always come in kind rather than cash. Again this is not the case in the United Kingdom.

All this makes an enormous difference to the politics of welfare reform on either side of the Atlantic. In the United States welfare has never been popular. The continued power of organised religion means the Protestant work ethic should not be underestimated. Most Americans believe the able-bodied poor could and should find work. Campaigning against welfare has always brought rich rewards for politicians. To a large extent this explains why President Clinton (under the influence of his then svengali Dick Morris) signed a welfare bill that many in the Democratic Party believed offended their most cherished principles. Despite holding a twenty-point lead over Robert Dole in the opinion polls, Clinton did not believe he could afford to be seen as pro-welfare. He wanted to be seen as pro-Medicare. He chose the terrain backed by the American middle class.

This cultural and political bias in favour of radical, even draconian, reform of welfare does not exist in the United Kingdom. The British public is hostile to those it believes exploit the system ('scroungers') but it shows no signs of outright antagonism to the concept of the welfare state in itself – and such attitudes would take a long time to shift. Those who doubt the validity of this analysis might consider the political fortunes of Mr John Moore, probably the only British cabinet minister in the 1980s to contemplate a radical assault on welfare. Alternatively, they might recall the reaction to John Major's short-lived back-to-basics campaign of the early 1990s which was characterised as an attack on single mothers.

Even allowing for the vast differences of structure and culture, further analytical problems abound. One is the size of area to be compared. Even if the Personal Responsibility Act was regarded as optimal legislation by British admirers, the United States as a whole must be regarded as too large for sensible analysis. This is the conclusion Republicans have drawn because much of their programme is designed to move decisions and resources away from Washington and towards the states. For some time policy innovation has been centred in the state capitals not Congress. The logical place for Britain to seek policy models is among those states sufficiently large to provide at least some basis for credible comparison.

A further complication lies in who receives welfare. To put it as delicately as one can, in the United States there is a very powerful relationship between the questions of race, lifestyles associated with race, the notion of an underclass and policy towards the poor. Americans on the left or right, politicians or the mass public in Washington and most larger states, work on the assumption that the average long-term welfare 'problem-case' is more often than not from the non-white community. Crude this sounds, this assumption, often made explicitly, does have some statistical validity behind it.

The legacy of slavery and segregation therefore haunts much of American social policy and casts a lengthy shadow over welfare. The relatively recent and rapidly expanding Hispanic population also has a specific set of problems associated with language and poverty. These factors affect liberal reformers (both black and white) as much as conservative radicals (again of either colour). It not only influences the nature of the debate but also the provisions passed into law. Any Anglo-American debate about the cultural ramifications of welfare soon reveals that while in the United States the whole issue is saturated with racial overtones, the same is not true for the United Kingdom. Given that race is such a potent issue in American welfare reform policy, British reformers should be extremely careful they are not proposing to replicate programmes designed for a very different society.

So, optimal policy comparison in this area involves a number of conditions. As stated earlier, the United Kingdom is best compared with state governments not the national model and the states need to be a certain size to make comparison meaningful. However, it would be more relevant if they also had a non-white population closer to that of the United Kingdom (5.5 per cent) rather than the corresponding figure in the United States (24.5 per cent). This is not a straightforward task as states which are disproportionately large tend (outside the Deep South) to also be disproportionately non-white. The selected states also need to have undertaken substantial welfare reform for a useful comparison to be made. Even bearing all this in mind, the earlier warnings about the differences between the structures and cultures of the two welfare systems still apply.

The dilemma can be illustrated simply. Let us take the twenty largest American states. If we exclude all states where non-white populations (as a proportion of the total) are more than 150 per cent of the figure for the United Kingdom only two (Wisconsin and Minnesota) remain. For the sake of wider choice, we might relax that condition and allow all states with non-white populations that are less than 200 per cent of the UK figures to remain in contention. That would leave four possible models for comfortable comparison: Massachusetts (but only just), Indiana, Wisconsin and Minnesota. Two of these states – Indiana and Minnesota – have not engaged in substantial welfare reform by recent American standards Massachusetts has to some degree and is worthy of study even if the non-white population is rather higher than the other three. This leaves Wisconsin. The state has indeed attracted intense attention from Britain's think tanks, academics, civil servants, elected officials and even journalists. So it should. But there are few other states from which relevant lessons can be drawn.

The simple conclusion is that the American welfare agenda needs to be handled with extreme caution by British Conservatives. There is a small number of states that could produce material that is worth investigating and which might (subject to a host of other structural/cultural challenges) be applicable in Britain. Wisconsin and (with more caution) Massachusetts should continue to be monitored by welfare reformers. If the citizens of Indiana and Minnesota ever elect individuals with new and interesting welfare agendas then attention here would be welcome as well. Some city-based projects could prove fruitful although size and race would both remain factors. The Personal Responsibility Act passed in Washington is therefore not especially helpful and would prove a false model if copied in Britain.

In the case of welfare, Conservatives might be better looking for other examples from overseas as well as the United States. The European Union itself is not a rich source of material but, in principle, Australia, Canada and New Zealand would be more worthwhile objects of study. Unfortunately, with the exception of some education and training reforms undertaken in Australia (which probably serve the Labour government better), neither it nor Canada has proved a hotbed of radicalism in this sphere. New Zealand has seen some extremely innovative changes in public policy that should interest British observers. However, the fact that it has the smallest population of these three countries might be considered a problem, though not necessarily an insuperable one. Nonetheless, one suspects that – with the partial exceptions of Wisconsin and Wellington – those in the Conservative Party who favour dramatic solutions to the problems of the welfare state will not find much through international comparison that will serve them usefully.

Crime: Even more Caution Required

Crime has long been as powerful a factor as economics and

welfare in explaining Republican political success on all levels in the United States. It was not surprising that measures to boost law and order occupied a central place in the Contract with America and continue to form a large proportion of the workload for the current Congress. Conservatives across the United States have favoured a tough approach towards law-breakers, and both the spirit and substance of that approach has already made a partial passage across the Atlantic due to the efforts of Michael Howard when he was at the Home Office. Conservatives may be tempted to look at the remaining Republican prospectus to complete the shift that Mr Howard began and the new Home Secretary Jack Straw seems likely to retain.

Republican proposals in this sector were no less radical than elsewhere. The exotically entitled Taking Back Our Streets Act covered several different initiatives. It favoured:

• A harder line on the death penalty. The Contract would drastically limit the ability of convicted killers to appeal against their execution. It has become commonplace for all manner of appeals to be launched with the consequence that fifteen years might pass between sentence and punishment. Extra funds would also be made available for states to prosecute these capital cases.

• Mandatory minimum sentences for drug crimes. The bill would create a compulsory minimum sentence of ten years for state or federal crimes that involved possession of a weapon. This would increase to twenty years after a second conviction and life imprisonment for a third offence.

• Mandatory victim retribution. This would ensure full

compensation by the perpetrator for the victims of crime for whatever financial loss was suffered as a result of the offence.

• Law enforcement block grants. This would have reversed the thrust of a 1994 bill identified with Bill Clinton by offering $10 billion over five years in general grants to local authorities to fund all law enforcement programmes. The Clinton-backed version had been more prescriptive about how local authorities should spend the money.

• Greater funds for prison construction. The federal government would make $10.5 billion available over a six-year period to finance state prison-building efforts. Receipt of funds was tied to how closely states followed through the sentences that had been handed down to violent criminals by their local judges. In particular, states should be able to demonstrate that at least 85 per cent of the sentence imposed on such individuals was actually served.

• Reform of the exclusionary rules. Republicans wanted to make it easier for the police to introduce evidence that had been obtained by means some would consider improper – without the correct search warrant for example – but where 'good faith' on behalf of the police could be demonstrated.

• Prisoners' rights. The Contract sought to limit the capacity of prisoners to sue their custodians over jail conditions. Many of these cases were regarded as frivolous or malicious and caused needless expense for the states concerned. In addition, a new process for deporting illegal immigrants found guilty of criminal offences was outlined, alongside new tracking procedures if such people attempted to enter the United States again.

• Stiffer penalties for crimes committed against children. A set of measures to implement harsher penalties was introduced as part of the separate Family Reinforcement Act.

Considering that many of these measures were overtly populist, it is surprising how few actually became law. The 1994 Crime Bill – associated with President Clinton – was not reversed. Indeed, nothing new of note emerged from this effort during the whole of 1995. In April 1996, Congress voted to attach a modified version of the limits on death penalty appeals to an Anti-Terrorism law that had been promoted in the aftermath of the Oklahoma bomb. Despite objections from liberal members of his administration, President Clinton signed this legislation. On the whole, though, for all its salience as a 'hot-button' issue to American life, Republicans did not manage a significant shift in federal policy towards crime despite their majority in both houses of Congress.

LESSONS FOR BRITAIN
The American prescription may seem sound to many Conservatives. The crime rate in Britain has soared at a relentless rate. Recent improvements cited by the Conservatives during the 1997 election campaign did not persuade the public that the situation had really changed. In an extraordinary switch, Tony Blair and Jack Straw were able to make partisan capital out of an issue that had long been political poison for their party. Tories might well be tempted to adopt an even tougher approach on crime to outflank their opponents and recapture this supremely sensitive issue.

However, substantial caution should be exercised for

similar reasons to those that apply to welfare. There are great dissimilarities in the nature of crime between the two nations. The recent position of the International Crime Victimisation Survey notwithstanding, the United States suffers from a far worse crime problem than the United Kingdom. This is especially true for the most violent forms of crime. According to the Federal Bureau of Investigation, a crime occurs every two seconds in the United States. That figure includes a violent crime every seventeen seconds, a property crime every three seconds, a robbery every fifty-one seconds, a forcible rape every five minutes and a murder every twenty-three minutes.

Not only are these figures appalling but until very recently they had been on a progressively worse course. Violent crime in the United States increased by 28.6 per cent between 1985 and 1994. Aggravated assault rose by 42 per cent in the same period, rape by 5 per cent and murder by 13.9 per cent. For reasons that are contestable and will be outlined shortly, crime has since receded on virtually all fronts since then but remains, in most American cities, at levels which the average citizen of the United Kingdom could barely comprehend.

Precisely because the crime rate is so striking, public authorities have resorted to solutions that could not be implemented in Britain. The death penalty, which was suspended by the Supreme Court during the mid-1970s, has come back with a vengeance since the Court relented in 1976. Some thirty-eight states now have the available techniques and death row has been filling rapidly across the nation. Regardless of the arguments for or against capital punishment, the well-established convention that it is an issue of conscience makes these provisions quite impractical as party policy in Britain.

Alongside execution, prison construction has boomed. The United States now has a prison population that exceeds one million people and which is likely to swell as a result of decisions taken at state and federal levels over the past five years. Much of the crime problem is related to drugs and the widespread availability of handguns. Firearms in America have never been anything like as prolific in the United Kingdom and the huge gap between the two countries and cultures will widen further if and when Labour succeeds in outlawing the ownership of virtually all handguns.

There are also important structural differences between the two nations that must be taken into account. Although Britain does not have a national police force in the sense that many European countries would understand, the thrust of Conservative legislation since 1979 has frequently served to narrow the regional distinctions between police forces. In contrast, law and order is radically decentralised in the United States. In much of rural America, policy is effectively delegated to the level of the sheriff. This structure has limited the ability of Congress to affect crime policy.

Republicans could not make up their minds whether they favoured more or even less centralisation. On the one hand they chose to allow states the luxury of block grants rather than accept the restrictions that went with the 1994 legislation. They also wanted to allow states more autonomy in areas such as the death penalty. On the other hand, Republicans sought to expand the number of cases that could be tried in the federal judicial system and wanted to attach conditions involving state prison sentencing practice to money made available for prison construction. This was not, frankly, the most coherent approach towards public policy in the Contract with America.

Once again this suggests that Washington DC is not the best place for Conservative reformers to start their examination of American initiatives. States or large cities would seem a much better prospect. This reintroduces the issue of size for the purpose of comparability. Furthermore, race is once again a matter of consideration. Although crime is not quite as powerfully affected by race as welfare, it has a substantial impact and does affect policy. Although black males constitute no more than 6 per cent of America's population, they now make up about half of the total prison population. On average, black Americans are around seven times more likely than their white counterparts to have been incarcerated in a state or federal prison. It should be noted that the clear majority of the victims of black crime are other black citizens – a fact that is rarely prominent in American political campaigning.

Even allowing for all these caveats and conditions, the United States is worth further analysis by Conservatives. As mentioned previously, this process was begun during Michael Howard's tenure as home secretary. Mr Howard, like the Republicans in Congress who framed the Taking Back Our Streets Act, appeared to be persuaded by what might be described as the 'California' approach to law and order. This works from the assumption that crime occurs because a hard core of career criminals has little fear of the judicial system.

Sentences are insufficiently long to deter them from offending. The solution is therefore to change the sentencing structure. This requires mandatory minimum sentences and a cumulative consequence to criminality such as the 'three strikes and you're out' philosophy. This was initially promoted by Governor Pete Wilson of California and then adopted by President Clinton, Speaker Gingrich and a host of others. A rapid expansion of prison places must, out of necessity, accompany this policy until criminals change their behaviour and the crime rate falls.

Many Conservatives have been impressed by this approach and would like to extend it further. But British Tories may not have awarded sufficient validity to an alternative strategy. This could be described as the 'New York' approach. It works on the assumption that what motivates career criminals is the belief that they are very unlikely to be caught, not that sentences will be unduly light in the unexpected event of arrest. Thus the solution to crime lies in reform of police attitudes and organisation to promote 'zero tolerance' of even the most minor violations. Once criminals are persuaded that their prospects of being caught are much higher than had hitherto been true, they will change their behaviour and the crime rate will diminish.

The most famous example of this technique occurred under Mayor Rudolph Guiliani and Commissioner William J. Bratton in New York City. Bratton took direct command of the City's ineffective 38,000 member force, held the seventy-six precinct commanders accountable for their performance in combatting crime in their areas, introduced high-technology into the fight against crime and fired those officers who would not adjust to the new system. Similar, if less dramatic examples, of police-centred approaches to law and order have been seen across the United States. Although the statistical evidence remains inconclusive at this stage, the New York school of action does appear to be outpacing its Californian rival in results. This fits in with common sense. Prospective criminals generally do not follow the course of penal policy in newspapers and journals. The arrival of mandatory sentences is probably not well known in the Los Angeles ghettos. The substantial extra presence of police officers, however, is likely to be noticed.

Conservatives in Westminster and Republicans in Washington have preferred California over New York. Both need to rethink their positions. Michael Howard has expressed rather less enthusiasm for zero tolerance than Jack Straw in recent years. But whether Mr Straw actually implements a zero tolerance policy is a different question. The American examples suggest that police reform is required to induce change in police practice. After the defeat of the Sheehy proposals in 1993, Michael Howard was reluctant to take on the British police and instruct them to reorganise in a manner that might result in more criminals being caught. There is no evidence that Mr Straw has any enthusiasm for another confrontation with the police either. If there is a lesson Conservatives could learn from their American cousins, it may well be that police reform not prison building might be more effective policy.

Conclusion

This paper has tried to outline the agenda followed by Republicans in Congress over the past two years and offer some analysis as to its applicability to Britain. This is not an entirely objective exercise. Public policy rarely is. Some commentators will disagree with the extent to which economic policy promoted on Capitol Hill by Republican politicians could form the core of a fresh Conservative approach in the House of Commons. Others will be less willing to allow issues of race to deter them from adopting American models of welfare reform. There will doubtless still be some who prefer Governor Pete Wilson of California over Mayor Rudolph Giuliani of New York as a crime fighter. Such differences are inevitable.

However, we hope the case we have outlined has achieved at least three of our objectives. First, that basic awareness of what Republicans proposed in the Contract with America will be increased. Second, that there is common ground on those aspects of the Contract that deal with issues so particular to the United States they cannot be considered relevant to Britain. Third, that although the margins between the respective domains might remain in dispute, the broad thrust of the argument offered here between economic initiatives, welfare reform and crime control is basically persuasive.

To sum up, on economic matters we believe that it is legitimate for British Conservatives to look at those measures passed at the federal level by Congress.

Furthermore, there are grounds for suspicion that a shift towards reforming tax allowances rather than cutting marginal rates might be the best course for Tories to follow. The pro-family and pro-growth bias of Republican tax policy should certainly be considered. On welfare reform it has been suggested that the states rather than Washington make for better comparison. A set of factors has been offered which implies that the number of states relevant for policy-makers in the United Kingdom is distinctly finite. On crime, even the states might not be the most appropriate level. American penal policy is generally located at a still more local level.

In none of these examples, even macroeconomics, should Conservatives simply convert dollars into sterling and then repeat the prescriptions that have been offered by Republicans in the House of Representatives. The search is for broad ideas not the fine print of legislation. The message we would like to offer is that some comparisons work better than others. The Conservatives, now cast into opposition in Britain, would do well to remember this as they look to the United States for fresh intellectual inspiration. The American agenda is certainly applicable in Britain. But success will depend on an appropriately sophisticated degree of selectivity from those who would go west for their next manifesto.

Papers in Print

Reports

3. Exiting the Underclass: Policy towards America's Urban Poor
Andrew Cooper, Catherine Moylan
£5.00

4. Britain's Borrowing Problem
Bill Robinson
£5.00

Occasional Papers

1. Deregulation
David Willetts
£3.00

2. 'There is No Such Thing as Society'
Samuel Brittan
£3.00

3. The Opportunities for Private Funding in the NHS
David Willetts
£3.00

4. A Social Market for Training
Howard Davies
£3.00

5. Beyond Unemployment
Robert Skidelsky, Liam Halligan
£6.00

6. Brighter Schools
Michael Fallon
£6.00

7. Understanding 'Shock Therapy'
Jeffrey Sachs
£8.00

8. Recruiting to the Little Platoons
William Waldegrave
£6.00

9. The Culture of Anxiety: The Middle Class in Crisis
Matthew Symonds
£8.00

Other Papers

Full Employment without Inflation
James Meade
£6.00

Memoranda

1. Provider Choice: 'Opting In' through the Private Finance Initiative
    Michael Fallon
    £5.00

2. The Importance of Resource Accounting
    Evan Davis
    £3.50

3. Why There is No Time to Teach:
    What is wrong with the National Curriculum 10 Level Scale
    John Marks
    £5.00

4. All Free Health Care Must be Effective
    Brendan Devlin, Gwyn Bevan
    £5.00

5. Recruiting to the Little Platoons
    William Waldegrave
    £5.00

6. Labour and the Public Services
    John Willman
    £8.00

7. Organising Cost Effective Access to Justice
    Gwyn Bevan, Tony Holland and Michael Partington
    £5.00

8. A Memo to Modernisers
    Ron Beadle, Andrew Cooper, Evan Davis, Alex de Mont,
    Stephen Pollard, David Sainsbury, John Willman
    £8.00

9. Conservatives in Opposition: Republicans in the US
    Daniel Finkelstein
    £5.00

10. Housing Benefit: Incentives for Reform
    Greg Clark
    £8.00

22. A Memo to Modernisers III
Evan Davis, John Kay, Alex de Mont, Stephen Pollard, Brian Pomeroy,
Katharine Raymond
£8.00

23. The Citizen's Charter Five Years On
Roderick Nye
£8.00

24. Standards of English and Maths in Primary Schools for 1995
John Marks
£10.00

25. Standards of Reading, Spelling and Maths for 7-year-olds in Primary Schools for 1995
John Marks
£10.00

26. An Expensive Lunch: The Political Economy of Britain's New Monetary Framework
Robert Chote
£10.00

Trident Trust/SMF Contributions to Policy

1. Welfare to Work: The *America Works* Experience
Roderick Nye (Introduction by John Spiers)
£10.00

2. Job Insecurity vs Labour Market Flexibility
David Smith (Introduction by John Spiers)
£10.00

Hard Data

1. The Rowntree Inquiry and 'Trickle Down'
Andrew Cooper, Roderick Nye
£5.00

2. Costing the Public Policy Agenda: A week of the *Today* Programme
Andrew Cooper
£5.00

3. Universal Nursery Education and Playgroups
Andrew Cooper, Roderick Nye
£5.00

4. Social Security Costs of the Social Chapter
    Andrew Cooper, Marc Shaw
    £5.00

5. What Price a Life?
    Andrew Cooper, Roderick Nye
    £5.00

Centre for Transition Economies: Papers

1. Russia's Stormy Path to Reform
    Robert Skidelsky (ed.)
    £20.00

2. Macroeconomic Stabilisation in Russia: Lessons of Reforms, 1992–1995
    Robert Skidelsky, Liam Halligan
    £10.00

Briefings

1. A Guide to Russia's Parliamentary Elections
    Liam Halligan, Boris Mozdoukhov
    £10.00